THROUGH THE VALLEY OF WEEPING

A 30-DAY DEVOTIONAL GUIDE ON WALKING
WITH JESUS THROUGH GRIEF, LOSS AND PAIN

MADELAINA ELIZABETH

*You're blessed when you feel you've
lost what is most dear to you.*

*Only then can you be embraced by
the One most dear to you."*

MATTHEW 5:4 MSG

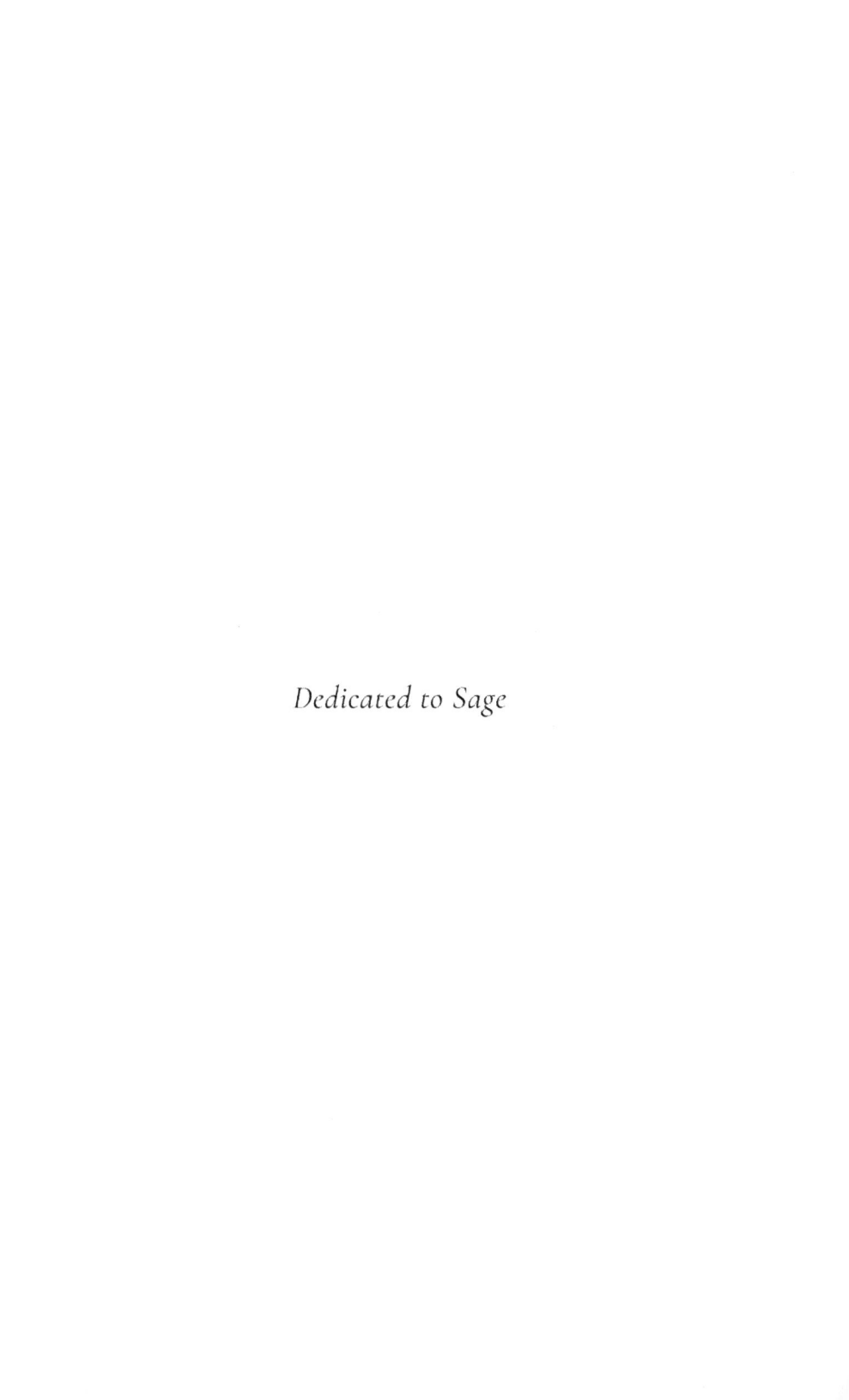

Dedicated to Sage

Dear Reader,

I've lost a lot, not just on a personal level but on a deep emotional level too. I've lost loved ones, I've lost a job, I've lost my health. Loss seems almost given in the human experience.

You may have lost a lot too. I know the feeling. When you're reeling, you don't know which way is up and you have no idea how you are going to get past the nightmare that has become your reality.

There is no other way through it but with Jesus. He is acquainted with our deepest grief (Isaiah 53:3). Only Jesus knows the depths of the pain you are experiencing and He is the only One who can walk through it with you to the other side. Like a Good Shepherd, He stays near to His sheep in the valley and leads them through it until they get to the other side.

I have walked through the valley of weeping, I know the footsteps on the path riddled with tear stains. I also have held the hand of my Savior through those dark valleys and it gave me the strength I needed to keep going. I made this devotional to help others walking through their valleys connect with the One who knows their heart. Jesus is with you in your darkest hour and is the only one who can infuse the light of hope.

These 30 days of devotionals are what God has spoken directly to me in my own quiet time as I have walked through challenge and pain. It is my hope that the words of comfort God has given me will also speak to you. My prayer is that this devotional guide blesses you, draws you closer to Jesus, and gives you the strength and hope you need to walk through this season with God.

Madelaina Elizabeth

Table of Contents:

DAY 1:
THROUGH THE VALLEY

I know the journey through this pain looks almost impossible. But I tell you, I am with you. You are walking through the valley and I am right here by your side. I see every tear, every moment of grief and breakdown, every bit of your struggle. I know what you are going through. And if I have led you into the Valley of Weeping, I will certainly lead you out to the heights of Zion where My glory dwells. I will guide you, all the way through.

O1   Look up Psalm 84:6-7 and write it here:

_____

_____

_____

_____

_____

O2   These verses paint a picture of walking through a valley and up a mountain (Zion) to meet God. Have you considered that your valley can lead you closer to Him? If not, how can you look at it now?

_____

_____

_____

O3   Psalm 84:6 promises the valley of weeping becomes a place of refreshing, where your pain can be transformed into a blessing for others. Write one way your valley can bless others, and hold onto that perspective today!

_____

_____

_____

_____

DAY 2:
JESUS IS HERE

I know this season has been hard between us and that it's been hard to come and talk to Me every day. I'm saddened by your struggles. Yet I am delighted you still have chosen to pursue Me, even today. I can't answer every single question you have all the time but keep coming to Me for answers. I want you to stay in relationship with Me because I want to be with you, even as you walk through this pain.

OI Look up Psalm 34:18 and write it here:

_____

_____

_____

_____

_____

Even if you have been feeling far from God, this Scripture assures us that God is in fact very near to us when we are hurting.

O2 Do you have a hard time being near to God this season? What are potential wrong beliefs about God that are keeping you from coming close to Him?

_____

_____

_____

_____

O3 Write a prayer to Jesus inviting Him back in to being close to you, asking Him to forgive you for any time you pushed Him away.

_____

_____

_____

_____

DAY 3:
IT'S ROOTED
IN HIS LOVE

The more you learn in this season to trust Me, the easier it will come to you for the rest of your life. Once you stop & become still, you'll soon see I have and am all that you need. From My perspective comes: although this season may be hard and painful, it's only temporary. And the most important thing becomes, not how high the pile of your pain is, but how deep the connection to My love becomes.

OI Look up Ephesians 3:17 and write it here:

_____

_____

_____

_____

_____

_____

02 How can the pain that you feel instead push you deeper into God's love?

_____

_____

_____

_____

_____

03 Take a moment and be still, closing your eyes and connecting to your breath. Focus yourself on receiving stillness, peace, comfort, reassurance, joy, delight and hope – all the fruits of God's love. Continue to try practicing that throughout your day.

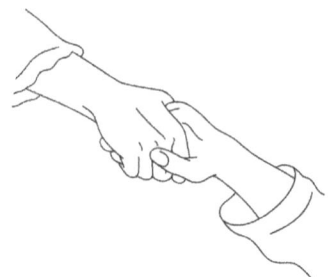

DAY 4:
GOD'S GOT YOU

If you feel like you are in too deep to get yourself out, that's when you rely on Me. If I allowed you into this mess, I surely can get you out. If it's longer than you expect — fine. But it's not longer than I have planned. I am sorry for the distress you are in. This is a time to hold Me more closely. Everyday choose to reach out to Me, I'm always here waiting. Despite the pain, despite the sorrow, come to Me. Do not let anything get in the way between Me and you.

OI Look up Psalm 40:2 and write it here:

_____

_____

_____

_____

_____

This Scripture promises that God is the one who lifts us out of the pit.

O2 Sometimes we put false expectations on ourselves to fix our pain when Jesus is reaching out to help us. What have you been putting on yourself that is a false expectation toward your healing?

_____

_____

_____

O3 Write a prayer of surrender to God releasing those expectations you have put on yourself and invite Jesus in to help lift you up.

_____

_____

_____

_____

_____

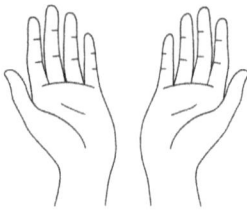

DAY 5:
WHAT IT IS ALL ABOUT

Lay down the distractions, lay down the doing and the striving and come to Me. Remember that My yoke is easy and My burden is light. Even in the depths of your pain, I am good. I am here. I am speaking. I am with you. This may not feel like reality but I promise you, it is. If all you get out of this season of pain is more of Me, would it be worth it? Does that make it all worth it? Doesn't coming to know your Savior face to face make every amount of loss and struggle fade away in the light of knowing Me? Your Creator, your Lord, your Savior? For I am the lover of your soul and I am your prize.

OI   Look up Philippians 3:8 and write it here:

_____

_____

_____

_____

02   How does "considering all things loss"
     compare to knowing Jesus shift your
     perspective on your current season?
     How are you coming to know Jesus
     better?

_____

_____

_____

_____

03   Write a prayer thanking Jesus for being
     present with you in this season. Tell Him
     how you want to know Him more, even
     in the midst of difficulty.

_____

_____

_____

_____

DAY 6:
WRITING A
BETTER STORY

I knew you from the beginning. In fact, I had your story written before it even started. I saw the pain, I saw the sorrow and the suffering and I made a heart of glory that could withstand the pressure. I am writing your story even now and it is filled with redemption and My goodness. I know how this story ends even if you don't. And trust Me, the ending is really good.

OI   Look up Psalm 139:16 and write it here:

_____

_____

_____

_____

_____

O2   This Scripture says that God wrote your story down before you were even born. How does that truth reframe your current season?

_____

_____

_____

_____

_____

O3   Write a prayer asking God to help you trust Him with the rest of your story and with the knowledge that the chapter ends exactly how He planned.

_____

_____

_____

_____

DAY 7:
HELD BY HIM

Come to Me dear one and let Me wash you besides the brooks of bliss. Let Me lead you gently, and be your constant companion. I am the shelter in your storm, the light that guides you in the dark. My dear one, I am here, I have not left. I have loved and love you through your most difficult times, I never gave up on you. When these days feel hard, forget not My benefits. For even in the fight, you are in My hands.

OI   Look up Psalm 139:10 and write it here:

---

02   How can you picture yourself being held in God's hands? How can that begin to feel like protection and rest, at the same time?

---

03   Whatever you answered above, go to that place and put it in your imagination. Throughout today, when you feel scared or lost or sad, put that image back in your imagination.

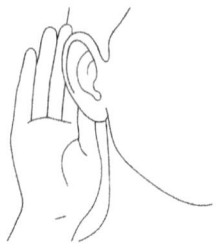

DAY 8:
YOU ARE HEARD

It is okay to hurt and be in pain. It is part of the human experience. You can give yourself permission to grieve. Sometimes holding onto all that emotion is more harmful. Letting it out and expressing your pain to Me and others is actually a helpful way to process what you are going through. And if you don't have anyone else to listen, remember I am always here as an attentive listening ear, a friend who is always eager to sit with you and hear your pain.

OI Look up Psalm 18:6 and write it here:

_____

_____

_____

This Scripture reminds us that God
hears our cries and listens intently to us.

O2 Where in your life are you holding back
emotion, thinking you need to stay
strong? What would it look like to tell
Jesus your pain instead?

_____

_____

_____

_____

O3 Write a prayer to Jesus releasing all the
pain you've been carrying. Let yourself
express every emotion you've been
holding onto.

_____

_____

_____

_____

DAY 9:
TO BE TRANSFORMED

Continue to allow Me to make you into My new creation and not only will your heart heal but you will experience a complete transformation, made entirely new. That is nothing less than what I already paid for on the cross. You will emerge from the chrysalis of suffering, and you will take flight into a new season. Your new colors on display for the whole world to see.

O1 Look up 2 Corinthians 3:18 and write it
here:

_____

_____

_____

_____

O2 Can you begin to view your current
valley season as a time of
transformation rather than just
hardship? In what ways might your pain
be shaping something new in you?

_____

_____

_____

_____

O3 List three areas of pain you're currently
experiencing. Next to each one, write
what you believe God could transform
that pain into. As you reflect, take a
moment to thank God for the hope He
gives that this is the beginning of
something new.

_____

_____

_____

_____

_____

DAY 10:
OVERFLOW

From this loss, you will learn a perspective of earth that only My dearest learn. To learn how to grieve and how to grow beyond it. The devil can try to steal, kill and destroy from you in this world but only you have the choice of how you respond. See this as an opportunity to get to know Me in ways only those in pain will ever understand. Because I, too, have been where you are and I want to help you heal. To be filled up with more of Me. And to let that dissipate every pain and sorrow.

O1   Look up 1 Peter 4:12-13 and write it here:

_____

_____

_____

_____

_____

_____

O2   This Scripture invites us to reframe how we view suffering and pain. It reminds us that in our trials, we have a unique opportunity to know Jesus more deeply by sharing in what He suffered. Can you think of an experience you are facing right now that feels similar to what Jesus endured?

_____

_____

_____

_____

_____

O3   Take a moment to reflect on how this experience can draw you closer to Jesus. When the pain or challenge arises today, pause, close your eyes, and thank Jesus for the privilege of getting to know Him more intimately through it.

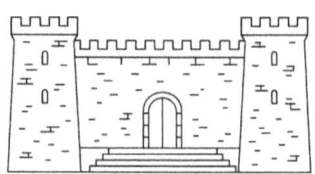

DAY 11:
PROTECTED
AND SHELTERED

You need not fear the arrows that fly by day or terrors of the night for I am your protector and your provider and you are certainly safe in My hands. Even if you feel a weapon has come against you, remember that no weapon formed against you will prosper. Meaning, I will strip away the impact of any weapon that comes against you and I will place you back on a firm foundation. Fear not, for I am the great redeemer and I can make all things right in the end.

OI Look up Psalm 91 and write it all here:

_____

_____

_____

_____

_____

_____

_____

_____

_____

_____

_____

_____

_____

_____

_____

_____

_____

_____

_____

This Scripture is the most well-known promise of God for our safety and protection. The Lord invites us not to define Him by our experiences but by the truth of His word. Even if you have not felt protected in the past, continue to come to Him and believe Him at His word. Pick one verse from Psalm 91 that resonates with you and commit to memorizing it.

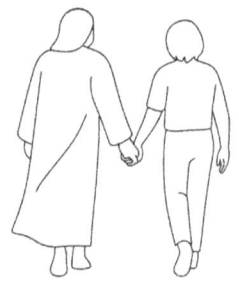

DAY 12:
YOU HAVEN'T
MISSED IT

You may feel that you have lost your way but I tell you, you are right on track. This journey may be long but you have not missed a step, for I have been guiding you all along even if you have not been aware of My presence. Surely I tell you, even now, I hold your hand and am guiding you to the end of this road. There is another side to this valley and you are growing closer and closer to its end. Keep trusting Me and keep going, I promise you it will be worth it.

OI   Look up Psalm 23:3-4 and write it here:

_____

_____

_____

_____

_____

This verse promises us that God guides us and God is near to us.

O2   Have you felt lost during this season? What does it make you feel to realize that even if you can't feel it, Jesus is still right beside you?

_____

_____

_____

_____

O3   God's goodness and plans are too big for us to get lost or miss; as long as our hearts are committed to Him. Write a prayer asking God to show you how near He is to you and how He has been with you all along, guiding you.

_____

_____

_____

_____

DAY 13:
BEAUTY FROM ASHES

I always turn ashes into beauty, even if you don't believe it right now. That is the beauty of following Me. I can do what you cannot. I can turn the greatest storm into your biggest blessing. Don't count out My ability to do the impossible. So when you begin to doubt, come to Me dear one. I have the answer and I know what I am doing. Keep your eyes fixed on Me and I will surely make a garden of beauty out of your pile of ashes.

01   Look up Isaiah 61:3 and write it here:

_____

_____

_____

_____

02   Do you believe that God can bring beauty out of your ashes? What may be limiting you from believing that He can do the impossible in your life?

_____

_____

_____

_____

_____

_____

03   Write out a prayer asking God to help renew your faith to believe that He will make beauty out of your ashes. Surrender to Him any unbelief that may be coming up.

_____

_____

_____

_____

DAY 14:
GOD IS SO
MUCH BIGGER

There is so much more of Me to learn. Even now, you are just scratching the surface. It would take many lifetimes to truly know Me and you can spend an eternity marveling. But now, you can honor Me by seeking Me in your pain. By choosing to trust Me despite your unanswered questions. I don't ask much of you, I just ask you to continue to learn how to trust Me, trust My word, trust My promises, and trust who I am. For I am so much bigger and better than you can imagine.

O1   Look up Proverbs 3:5-6 and write it here:

_____

_____

_____

_____

_____

O2   There is so much about God we don't know, great mysteries we may never understand this side of Heaven. What question in your heart might be keeping you from trusting God more deeply?

_____

_____

_____

_____

O3   Write a prayer of surrender to God offering up the question you've been holding onto. Ask Him to give you new grace to trust Him more.

_____

_____

_____

_____

_____

DAY 15:
JESUS IS
YOUR ANCHOR

All you can do is stay anchored in Me. Through the ups and downs, through the good days and bad, life comes in waves. It's okay to have harder days than others. When those hard days come, give yourself grace and hold onto Me. I am with you in this. Even on your worst day, I am there with you, holding onto you and keeping you steady. Our connection is what secures you into the depths of understanding Me.

OI   Look up Hebrews 6:19 and write it here:

_____

_____

_____

_____

_____

_____

The hope for our souls is Jesus!

O2   What might holding onto Jesus as your anchor look like for you?

_____

_____

_____

_____

O3   Write a prayer asking God to show you opportunities to help you cling to Jesus this week when circumstances arise that feel uncertain or overwhelming.

_____

_____

_____

_____

_____

DAY 16:
HE KNOWS YOUR GRIEF

It is okay to hurt. You do not need to muster up your own strength to force yourself into joy. Pain creates grief and I understand the days where the relief of joy feels too far away. That is because I am acquainted with the deepest grief. I have been where you are, I understand the pain you are going through. This isn't about anything or anyone else but Me and you. Lock eyes with Me, come closer to Me. I will be the one who gets you through this season of difficulty.

01 Look up Isaiah 53:3-4 and write it here:

02 These verses tell the story of Jesus' suffering and the weight of suffering He carried on the cross – including yours. What are some ways you can release your sorrow and weakness to Jesus?

03 Take a moment to imagine Jesus on the cross, carrying your sorrow. Lock eyes with Him in your imagination and try to feel how much He understands your pain. Remember you are not alone. Take this encounter into your day today.

DAY 17:
CROWNED IN GLORY

In this trial of fire, see how you are emerging; see who is coming out. I like that person a lot, that is who I wanted to see emerge your whole life. Let the pressure transform you into the diamond that you are. Where you become a person molded into My image, deeply shaped into someone who walked with me through the fire. You will come out on the other side of this, refined by fire and made into solid gold.

OI   Look up James 1:12 and write it here:

_____

_____

_____

_____

02   Fire and pressure form gold and diamonds, the elements that make a crown. What are the metaphorical gold and diamonds God is forming in you during this season of fiery trial?

_____

_____

_____

_____

_____

03   Imagine how what God is forming in you could be rewarded as your own "crown of life." Write down the answers you came up with.

_____

_____

_____

_____

DAY 18:
A PATH THAT
FINDS YOU

You have not missed a step on this journey through the valley that you are walking. It is because My steps meet you. This path is not as linear as you think. It is a path that finds you, goes along with you, nudging you in the right direction as you go. I am much bigger than you think, surrounding you with every step you take. So keep walking and know My love meets you right where you are.

OI Look up Isaiah 30:21 and write it here:

_____
_____
_____

This verse depicts a scenario where God is standing so close to someone that He is whispering instructions on where to walk.

O2 This is a new way to imagine walking with God; not where He harshly pushes you one way or another, but where He gently guides you. Where in your life do you sense God whispering direction even if the path isn't clear or linear?

_____
_____
_____
_____
_____

O3 Write a prayer asking Jesus to help you trust His guidance more on your journey.

_____
_____
_____
_____

DAY 19:
DAWN ALWAYS COMES

Look around you, nighttime is not just a moment but for a half a day. You must wait until dawn breaks. But assuredly, dawn always comes. Let that be a promise, that no matter how scary and lonely and difficult this night season is, the sun will always rise. Let the dawning of a new day fill you with the rays of hope. So keep holding My hand in the dark and let the light of a new day rise upon you.

OI   Look up Isaiah 60:1 and write it here:

_____

_____

_____

_____

_____

_____

O2   Do you feel stuck in your night season? How can you remind yourself that the night doesn't last forever?

_____

_____

_____

_____

_____

_____

O3   Step outside today (or when it's sunny out) and take in the sunlight on your face. Think of Isaiah 60:1 and take in the sunlight as a reminder that God's light rises to shine on you!

DAY 20:
A SWEET FEAST
IS PREPARED

I can make the bitter waters sweet. Whatever bitterness that has marked this season of tears, I will wipe away and turn those tears into a sweet stream of beauty. Whatever has been salty and bitter to your taste will turn into My sweet goodness. Remember that I prepare a feast for My loved ones and it is a feast filled with good things and good gifts.

01 Look up Psalm 34:8 and write it here:

02 Have you felt like life has handed you a
    bitter cup? What are the areas in your
    life right now that you want sweetened?

03 Write a prayer inviting Jesus to sweeten
    those bitter places, ask Him help you
    truly taste and see that He is good, even
    in this season.

DAY 21:
THE GIFT OF
LONGSUFFERING

Longsuffering is what caused My gospel to spread across the earth. Longsuffering is a Godly value that can take you far with Me. Longsuffering is a fruit of the Spirit that can get you through anything. It gives you the strength you need to stand in the gap for Heaven to come to earth. You may feel you are suffering for no reason but I tell you, the fruit of longsuffering being developed in you is for greater Kingdom works.

OI Look up Galatians 5:22 and write it here:

_____

_____

_____

_____

Notice this Scripture says "patience", or "longsuffering" in some translations, is a fruit of the Spirit

O2 Where in your life are you experiencing longsuffering right now? How do you think developing this fruit could serve greater Kingdom purposes in the future?

_____

_____

_____

O3 Write a prayer asking Jesus to show you new perspectives of what He can do with the longsuffering you develop in this season. Ask Him to fill your heart with hope that what you are going through now will be used for His good.

_____

_____

_____

_____

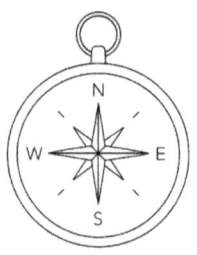

DAY 22:
GOD KNOWS
THE DIRECTION

Center yourself in who I am and what I can give you. Stop trying to look around and predict what's coming. Honestly, usually you are right but also wrong. Because what you see are vague, foggy shapes ahead in the midst. What I can see are the tiny, exact minuscule details before, ahead & behind you. You are not able to see from My perspective. And that's okay because you need to trust that I can see. I, the Father, see more than you, from Heavenly heights compared to earthly lows. And so, it becomes an exercise of faith to surrender into My hands exactly My way and My plans.

O1   Look up Isaiah 55:9 and write it here:

_____

_____

_____

_____

O2   Are there situations right now where things feel unclear or "foggy"? How does this Scripture and message change your perspective to those uncertainties?

_____

_____

_____

_____

O3   Take a moment to imagine all your plans, expectations and worries you have for your direction in life. Now picture yourself putting them into a box and handing them to Jesus. Receive the freedom He gives back to you. Soak that today!

DAY 23:
HOPE IS AHEAD

There is so much ahead for you. Full and complete healing, freedom and joy. I see your pain even today. It's going to be okay. This won't last, this won't be forever. There is a bright horizon ahead of you if you only wait out the night a little longer. I have not forgotten you, I see you, I see your hardships and I most certainly will redeem what has been lost. There are many people who have had pain in their life and walked through it with Me. And that pain has developed character. That is what I want to do in you. Now I want you to lean into the mystery of how character leads to hope. Because hope is what I have for you.

01 Look up Romans 5:4 and write it here:

_____

_____

_____

_____

02 This Scripture connects the dots from trials (Romans 5:3) to endurance to character which all lead to hope. What do you think might be one of the Divine mysteries hidden in that process?

_____

_____

_____

_____

03 Write a prayer thanking God in advance for the hope He is bring to you. Even if you don't feel it yet, choose to trust that hope is coming.

_____

_____

_____

_____

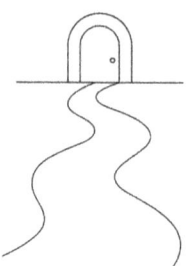

DAY 24:
THE ROAD TO LIFE

All you need to do is keep walking down this road. A lot of what you want is ahead of you. You just need to keep going and have patience. Your pain needs to be healed before more is added. Keep focusing on Me, keep putting one foot in front of another. This is a hard road but the narrow road always leads to better places; it leads to life.

OI Look up Matthew 7:14 and write it here:

_____

_____

_____

_____

O2 What does the "narrow road" look like in your life right now and how can you look at it to see it as a path to true life?

_____

_____

_____

_____

O3 Write a prayer asking God to strengthen you as you walk this narrow road. Invite Him to heal the parts of your heart that are still hurting, and to renew your hope for what's ahead.

_____

_____

_____

_____

_____

DAY 25:
YOU WILL RISE UP

You have so much more strength than you know. Not anyone could go through this season and handle it like you are. You have chosen to put the energy of heartbreak into the right direction. Not everyone understands the depths of pain you are in, but I do because I have been there too. I have been to the depths of Sheol and I have risen out victoriously. And so will you, rising up on wings like eagles.

OI Look up Isaiah 40:31 and write it here:

_____

_____

_____

_____

_____

Just as Jesus rose up from the grave, the promise of Isaiah 40 can be seen as our own promise of resurrection, rising up in new strength.

O2 Do you need new strength today? What might it look like for God to give you new strength?

_____

_____

_____

_____

_____

O3 Imagine the Holy Spirit filling you up with new strength and what it feels like to soar high, lighter than before. Ask God to help you continue to keep that feeling with you today.

DAY 26:
THE FOUNDATION
OF LOVE

Build back on a foundation of My love. Yes, metaphorical destruction has come into your life but I never intended your story to end here. I always build back better. Now, I want My love to be the rock that everything else in your life is built on. I want you to see Me as I really am, a loving Father who so loved the world that I sent you a Savior, an answer to all your pain. My love compels Me and My love is what sustains all life. Let My love hold you and sustain you, let My love wash over you and slowly melt away every ounce of sadness and pain.

OI Look up Ephesians 3:17-18 and write it here:

_____

_____

_____

_____

02 How can you build back from this season on the foundation of God's love? What can you do now to start doing that?

_____

_____

_____

_____

_____

03 Write a prayer asking God to help you focus on His love today and to help show you ways you can build back on His foundation of love.

_____

_____

_____

_____

_____

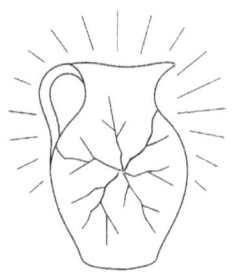

DAY 27: WORKING ALL THINGS TOGETHER FOR GOOD

Give to Me your pain and let Me turn it into something beautiful. That's what I do and who I am. I am your redeemer, I take the broken and make it whole again, infusing into those broken places My glory so that where you have experienced pain, you will now shine My light of love out into the world. Take heart and trust who I am and who I have been to you.

OI   Look up Romans 8:28 and write it here:

_____

_____

_____

_____

Remember that God is able to take even the worst situation and turn it into good for His purposes.

O2   How might your current pain be preparing you to shine His love to others?

_____

_____

_____

_____

O3   Write a prayer inviting Jesus to show you new ways of how your pain and lead to a bigger purpose with God.

_____

_____

_____

_____

_____

DAY 28:
THERE IS JOY COMING

I see your tears dear one, I see all that you have lost. I sit with you in your pain, I acknowledge the weeping that lasts throughout the night. I even know the number of tears that have fallen down your face just as much as I know the number of hairs on your head. I will certainly redeem all that you have lost. For you have put your trust in Me, the maker of Heaven and earth. And My redemption will bring you the fullness of joy, because joy comes in the morning, where you will see what I can do with a bottle full of tears and a hand that works it all for good.

OI   Look up Psalm 30:5 and write it here:

A wise teacher taught that joy comes when God moves and answers our prayers; it's connected to something tangible.

O2   What would God's redemption look like for you coming out of this season? How could that make it feel like joy has come in the morning?

O3   Write a declaration that God's redemption is coming for you, be specific with what you answered above.

DAY 29:
THE PRIZE THAT
OUTWEIGHS IT ALL

Hold onto the promise that what you are going through will end and it will produce in you a glory that vastly outweighs everything. It will be an eternal glory, one that no one can ever take from you. Is it not the prize you have been searching for anyway? Always remember that I am able to restore you and place you back on a firm foundation once this season of testing is done.

01　Look up 1 Peter 5:10 and write it here:

_____

_____

_____

_____

God's promise to restore, support, strengthen and put us on a firm foundation – even if it doesn't feel like this season of hardship will end.

02　What are ways you are able to remind yourself today that God will bring closure to this season and place you back on a firm foundation?

_____

_____

_____

_____

_____

03　Take those ways you brainstormed and put them into action. Commit to memory the promise of this verse.

DAY 30:
THE MORNING
STAR OF HOPE

It's all ahead for you, My promises redeemed and restored. Will you wait out the night a little longer? Will you fix your eyes on the horizon, in anticipation that the sun will soon appear? A first like a small sliver of hope and then soon, like a blazing emblem of glory; assuring you that the night season was only temporary and that day always shines brighter. I am the Morning Star and I will surely bring My light into your new day.

OI Look up Revelation 22:16 and write it here:

_____

_____

_____

_____

_____

02 What does Jesus being the "Morning Star" mean to you? How can you look ahead for your life and see it with hope?

_____

_____

_____

_____

_____

_____

03 God's assurance to us is that the night season is only temporary, a valley we are just passing through. Take a moment and imagine how you can picture this season as temporary. Hold onto that picture today and any time you may feel stuck.

FINAL THOUGHTS

I pray that these 30 days have been reassuring and refreshing to you and that you are closer to Jesus than when you started. I hope that God has spoken directly to you through these messages and Scriptures and that you have become confident that He is near to you in your pain and that this valley won't last forever.

I pray that these 30 days gave you what you needed to stay close to God in your time of need. I would encourage you to keep going to Him even now that you're finished with this devotional. Keep praying, keep journaling and keep reading your Bible. If there were any specific days that really resonated with you, bookmark them and go back to them when you are feeling down. Keep surrounding yourself with reminders that God is with you and you will walk through this season victoriously.

Most importantly I leave with you this — weeping may last through the night but joy comes in the morning. Your morning will come and your heart will once again be filled with joy. All because the Jesus we walk with is good and faithful to His word.

So keep going through this valley with your Good Shepherd Jesus and you will walk out the other side and see the bright light of morning break like dawn.

Madelaina Elizabeth

ABOUT ME

It is my joy to be able to publish this devotional guide to help others who are walking through their own valleys. It is a glimpse of how God takes what the enemy meant for evil and turns it for good.

I wrote this devotional because when I was walking through a hard season, I needed help connecting with God in the midst of my pain. I hope this devotional can be that answer for others looking for help.

I live in sunny Redding, CA, with my sister-best friend and my three cats. I enjoy hiking, paddleboarding, running, gardening, writing and cooking. I published my first book, another devotional, in 2023 and have been blown away by its reception. I continue to be excited for all the opportunities yet to come with my writing!

Looking for More
Faith-Filled Encouragement?

Follow along and read
more on my blog:

Check out my first
devotional, "Living in
God's Fullness"

www.madelainaelizabeth.com

"Deepening in faith and flourishing in life"

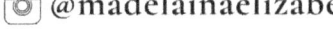 @madelainaelizabeth

_____

If the book cover spoke to you, you'll find
even more encouraging, Spirit-led art at
Barnabé Studio's Etsy shop:

BARNABÉ STUDIO
www.barnabestudio.com